PARALLEL UNIVERSES

EXPLAINED

THE MYSTERIES OF SPACE

PARALLEL UNIVERSES
EXPLAINED

RYAN JEFFREY FARBER

Enslow Publishing
101 W. 23rd Street
Suite 240
New York, NY 10011
USA

enslow.com

Published in 2019 by Enslow Publishing, LLC.
101 W. 23rd Street, Suite 240, New York, NY 10011

Library of Congress Cataloging-in-Publication Data

Names: Farber, Ryan Jeffrey, author.
Title: Parallel universes explained / Ryan Jeffrey Farber.
Description: New York : Enslow Publishing, [2019] | Series: The mysteries of space | Audience: Grades 7 to 12.
Identifiers: LCCN 2018015001| ISBN 9781978504578 (library bound) | ISBN 9781978505582 (pbk.)
Subjects: LCSH: Multiverse—Juvenile literature. | Cosmology—Juvenile literature. | Quantum theory—Juvenile literature.
Classification: LCC QB983 .F37 2018 | DDC 523.1—dc23
LC record available at https://lccn.loc.gov/2018015001

Printed in the United States of America

To Our Readers: We have done our best to make sure all websites in this book were active and appropriate when we went to press. However, the author and the publisher have no control over and assume no liability for the material available on those websites or on any websites they may link to. Any comments or suggestions can be sent by email to customerservice@enslow.com.

Photo Credits: Cover GiroScience/Shutterstock.com; p. 5 d1sk/Shutterstock.com; p. 7 Basti Hansen/Shutterstock.com; p. 8 Juergen Faelchle/Shutterstock.com; p. 12 Vadim Sadovski /Shutterstock.com; p. 14 ktsdesign/Shutterstock.com; p. 17 Science Photo Library /Alamy Stock Photo; p. 18 Science History Images/Alamy Stock Photo; p. 21 Getty Images; p. 23 Keystone-France/Gamma-Keystone/Getty Images; pp. 25, 64 Designua/Shutterstock.com; p. 28 NASA/Wmap Science Team/Science Photo Library/Getty Images; pp. 32, 57 Mark Garlick /Science Photo Library/Getty Images; p. 34 Rick Friedman/Corbis Historical/Getty Images; p. 35 Roman Sigaev/Shutterstock.com; p. 38 David Neff/Corbis News/Getty Images; p. 43 Fouad A. Saad/Shutterstock.com; p. 44 Mehau Kulyk/Science Photo Library/Getty Images; p. 47 Richard Kail/Science Photo Library/Getty Images; p. 49 Sam Ogden/Science Source; p. 53 SPL/Science Source; p. 55 Robert Brook/Science Photo Library/Getty Images; p. 59 Peter Macdiarmid/Getty Images; p. 66 fotosutra/Shutterstock.com; p. 67 Nicolle R. Fuller /Science Source; back cover and interior pages sdecoret/Shutterstock.com (Earth's atmosphere from space), clearviewstock/Shutterstock.com (space and stars).

CONTENTS

INTRODUCTION

Earth is one of many planets in the solar system. From scorching sun-facing Mercury to the frigid abode of Neptune, a total of eight planets orbit the sun. Scientists have even discovered planets orbiting other stars. Space telescopes have found sizzling-hot Jupiter-like planets orbiting six times closer to their star than Mercury, "puff-ball" planets with atmospheres much bigger than their rocky cores, and water worlds. Although planet hunters have found a few thousand planets, they're still looking for a "second Earth." Astronomers expect there to be planets around most of the one hundred billion stars in the Milky Way galaxy, so there are still billions of planets waiting to be discovered!

Our home, the Milky Way, is also one of many galaxies. From itty-bitty dwarf galaxies to the behemoth, brightest cluster galaxies, from bright blue spiral galaxies to red-and-dead fossil galaxies, astrophysicists have seen more than ten thousand galaxies in a single snapshot from the Hubble Space Telescope. Astronomers expect there may be as many as one trillion galaxies in the universe.

What about the universe? Is our home universe all alone? Or do other parallel universes exist? One of the first scientific theories of parallel universes used Albert Einstein's theory of relativity.

This is the Milky Way galaxy as seen from Earth. Since Earth is inside the Milky Way, one sees a "milky" band of stars lying in the plane of the galaxy.

The astounding discovery of gravitational waves in 2015 made by LIGO (the Laser Interferometer Gravitational-Wave Observatory) validated Einstein's theory of relativity with the strongest possible evidence. Wormholes are an application of relativity that remain unproven. But interestingly, one parallel universe theory suggests that black holes may actually be wormholes, connecting the universe to parallel universes.

A simpler parallel universe theory stems directly from evidence supporting the big bang theory. Observations of the extraordinary flatness of the universe suggest that a near infinite number of parallel universes likely exist just beyond the horizon of the universe.

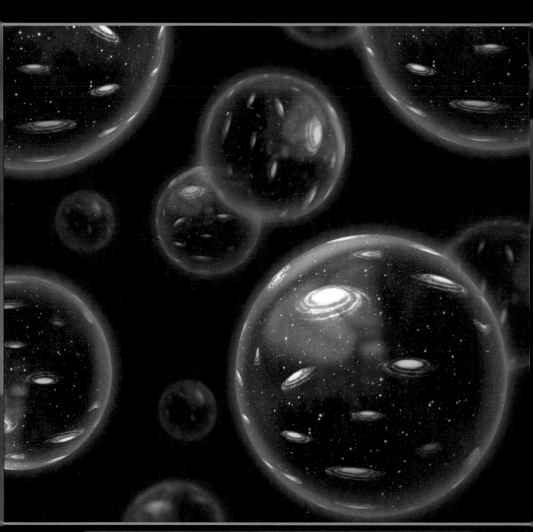

An artistic rendering of the multiverse shows each universe represented by a bubble and filled with galaxies. The nearest universe may be lying relatively nearby as in this image, or it may be nearly infinitely far away.

While puzzles continue to plague the standard big bang theory, the addition of inflation naturally resolves these problems. Furthermore, inflation suggests the existence of the multiverse, in which the universe is but one bubble in a cosmic bubble bath.

From black holes to the big bang, Einstein's theory of relativity can explain large-scale happenings in the universe. Yet, relativity breaks down at the smallest scales. Nearly every event on Earth, from the friction that enables ice skaters to pirouette to the beating of a drum at a rock concert, relies on the strange physics of quantum mechanics. One bizarre interpretation of quantum mechanics states that for every choice one makes, the universe splits into two parallel universes.

Strange and stranger still, the concept of hyperspace supposes there exist unseen higher dimensions. Why believe in these higher dimensions if they cannot be seen? An easy explanation exists for how light can wave in empty space, provided there exists a fifth dimension. The notion of higher dimensions suggests that parallel universes may be like pages in a book, lying just beyond one's reach.

The holy grail of physics, the last wish of Einstein, is a theory of everything. Superstring theory postulates that astronomically miniscule strings are the most basic building block of the universe. Unified superstring theory requires the existence of eleven dimensions, of which there may be two more three-dimensional universes.

Though many questions remain, it is evident that since the time of Einstein, ideas of parallel universes have grown from far-out concepts to mature scientific theories.

Chapter One

Wormholes in Space-time

Once upon a time, there lived a town on a piece of binder paper. A smattering of houses and stores, owned and operated by paper people, filled the paper world. Papias was a particularly popular paper child. Papias lived in Paper Town, next door to the ice cream store and near the top hole punch. The three "punch holes" were considered wonders of the world. Paper people from all four edges of the paper world traveled to see the punch holes. Many explorers, desiring to know where they might lead, jumped into the punch holes. Yet none of the explorers ever returned to Paper Town. The mayor of Paper Town ordered an investigation to determine if the explorers might yet return. After many studies, the leading scientists of the day declared punch holes were bottomless abysses and advised against any new exploration.

While Papias enjoyed living near the ice cream store and the northern punch hole, the only school in Paper Town was many lines to the south, near the southern punch hole. Papias had to wake up very early to walk to school on time. One night Papias fell asleep in bed, wondering what may lay at the bottom of a punch hole. "Is there even a bottom?" Papias wondered, drifting off to sleep.

"Ring-ring-ring!" sounded the school bell's five-minute warning. Papias forgot to set an alarm! Papias leaped out of bed, grabbed a paper backpack, and dashed out the door. But after a few steps, Papias suddenly stopped. There was no way to make it to school on time.

"Fear not!" thundered a booming voice, seeming to sound from the four corners of the paper world. After a short pause, Paper Town shaked and quaked, knocking Papias to the ground. "For I have given unto thee a shortcut. Jump into the punch hole and all will be well."

Papias thought back to the scientists' warnings that punch holes were bottomless abysses from which no one returned. Yet the voice sounded strangely familiar. With a brave sense of adventure, Papias leaped into the punch hole by the ice cream store and found the school directly ahead! Papias walked in and sat down just as the final bell rang. As the teacher blathered something incomprehensible about Einstein-Rosen bridges, Papias wondered about the journey into the punch hole. What did that voice do?

The voice, a human being, simply folded the piece of paper in half width-wise. In doing so, the top and bottom hole punches were linked together. In this example, a wormhole connected two distant parts of the paper world, providing a shortcut. However, if the voice were a prankster, stapling two pieces of paper together, then Papias would have arrived in a parallel paper world.

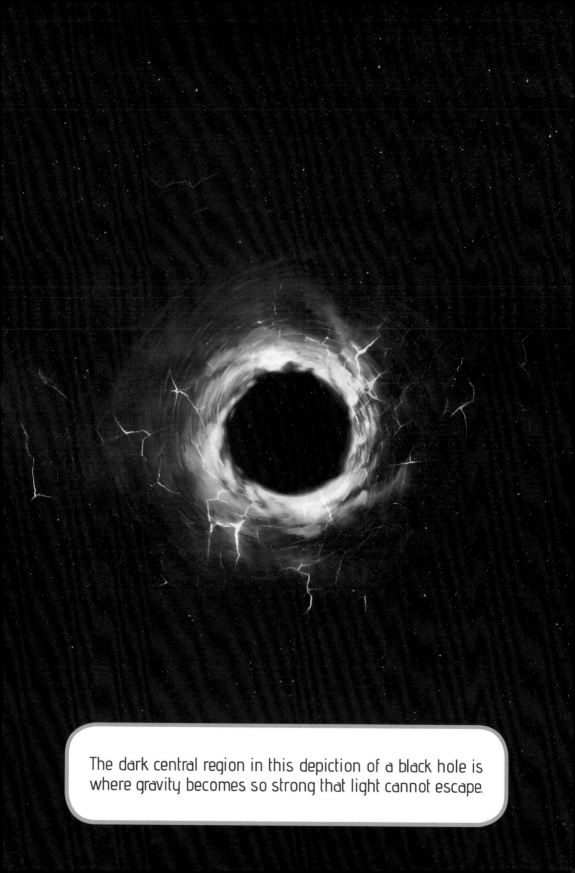

The dark central region in this depiction of a black hole is where gravity becomes so strong that light cannot escape.

The punch holes in this story represent black holes. A black hole is a region in space where gravity is so strong that not even light can escape.[1] What happens to something once it falls into a black hole? Just as the paper people were led to believe that punch holes were "bottomless abysses," so too are the insides of black holes commonly regarded as "boring" places. What goes into a black hole does not come back out. However, it is possible that black holes may actually be wormholes, providing shortcuts in space, acting as time machines, or even enabling travel to a parallel universe. To understand why this may be, one must learn a bit more about wormhole theory.

Black Holes and White Holes

In 1915, Albert Einstein (1879–1955) finished crossing the T's in his theory of relativity, declaring the speed of light to be the speed limit of the universe and updating the laws of gravity. Twenty years later, Einstein's assistant Nathan Rosen (1909–1995) had a daring idea. Rosen ingeniously discovered that wormholes were valid solutions to the equations of relativity.[2] These solutions, called Einstein-Rosen bridges in honor of their discoverers, required white holes to exist for every black hole. A white hole is the polar opposite of a black hole. A white hole spits out everything that its twin black hole swallows up. Much as nothing can escape from a black hole, nothing can enter a white hole. In this way, Einstein-Rosen bridges are one-way wormholes; they are more akin to sliding down a fireman's pole than walking across a bridge.

Unfortunately, the simple wormhole of an Einstein-Rosen bridge in Einstein's relativity will never enable weekend vacations to a parallel universe. In 1962, astrophysicists John Archibald

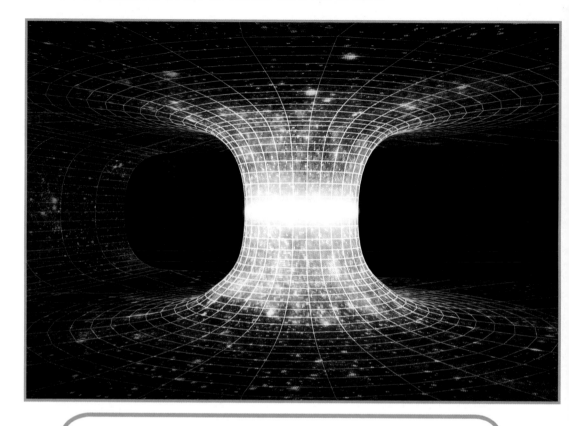

This is a conceptual visualization of an Einstein–Rosen bridge, or wormhole. Space is warped more and more strongly as one approaches the wormhole, at some point tunneling through to a distant part of the universe or to a parallel universe.

Wheeler (1911–2008) and Robert W. Fuller (1936–) showed that Einstein-Rosen bridges are unstable, collapsing too quickly for anything more than a particle to get through.[3] So are wormholes a lost cause? Not quite.

Traversing a Wormhole

More than one hundred years after Einstein completed his theory of relativity, scientists still use that original theory to predict and

WORMHOLES IN THE MARVEL CINEMATIC UNIVERSE

Wormholes have been featured prominently in science fiction, from *Star Trek* to the Marvel Cinematic Universe. Why are sci-fi fans wormhole lovers? Since faster-than-light travel is impossible under Einstein's theory of relativity, the only physically consistent way to travel across the galaxy, or the entire universe, is to use a wormhole. A recent case of wormhole heroism occurred in *Thor: Ragnarok* (2017). Warning! Spoilers ahead. To return home from the gladiator world of Sakaar, Thor, Valkyrie, and Banner launched their spaceship into a wormhole. Banner described the wormhole as a collapsing neutron star within an Einstein-Rosen bridge. Banner was largely correct, since neutron stars that get too heavy collapse to form black holes. In the real universe, scientists debate whether wormholes connect parallel universes or merely distant points in the same universe together.

understand many phenomena, including gravitational waves. Although the original theory is the most mainstream version, a few alternatives exist. In 1922, physicist Élie Cartan (1869–1951) modified relativity to let space twist.[4]

Think of space as a towel. Imagine two people holding the towel taut. If a heavy ball is rolled on the towel, the towel bends, just as space does in the presence of a heavy black hole. If one person shakes the towel, it can send waves rippling through, like gravitational waves rippling through space. Now suppose the towel was wet. To get the water out, the two people would twist opposite corners. The result is a (very) twisted space.

Cartan included the twisting and untwisting of space when he modified Einstein's theory of relativity, which is called Einstein-Cartan theory. Einstein-Cartan theory was largely forgotten until the 1960s. Researchers, disappointed that Wheeler and Fuller proved wormholes were unstable in Einstein's original formulation of relativity, searched for a loophole. Dennis Sciama (1926–1999) and Tom Kibble (1932–2016) independently rediscovered Einstein-Cartan theory—the wormhole loophole.[5,6] Today, astrophysicists use Einstein-Cartan-Sciama-Kibble theory to better understand the big bang—as well as wormholes.

The ability of space to twist in Einstein-Cartan theory provides a way for wormholes to be stable (Wheeler and Fuller's unstable wormholes were twist-free). Einstein-Cartan theory predicts wormholes form during the birth of new black holes. These wormholes may connect our universe to parallel universes. It's even possible that our universe's big bang was actually a white hole. In other words, our universe was born when a pre-existing, or "parent," universe formed a black hole.

Do White Holes Really Exist?

The idea that the big bang may have been a white hole is jaw-dropping. But are white holes some bizarre idea floating inside astronomers' brains? Has anyone seen a white hole in our universe? Perhaps. On June 14, 2006, a dazzlingly bright burst of gamma rays (light even more dangerous than UV or X-rays)

White holes spit out matter, such as gas and dust, and are impossible to enter.

flooded the heavens for 102 seconds.[7] Swift, a NASA satellite, detected the gamma-ray burst (GRB060614) and sounded its alarm, waking up groggy astronomers around the world. As swiftly as they could, astronomers threw coats over their pajamas and ran off to their telescopes. And though they peered through the eyepieces of the largest telescopes in the world and even phoned their friend Hubble up in space, they simply became more puzzled the more they learned.

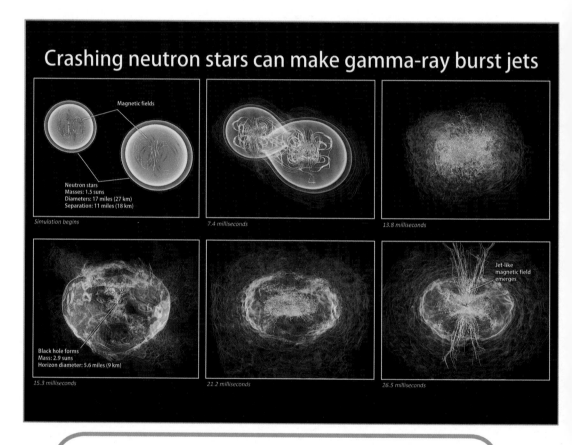

Crashing neutron stars can make gamma-ray burst jets

Magnetic fields

Neutron stars
Masses: 1.5 suns
Diameters: 17 miles (27 km)
Separation: 11 miles (18 km)

Simulation begins

7.4 milliseconds

13.8 milliseconds

Black hole forms
Mass: 2.9 suns
Horizon diameter: 5.6 miles (9 km)

15.3 milliseconds

21.2 milliseconds

Jet-like
magnetic field
emerges

26.5 milliseconds

A supercomputer simulation shows neutron stars, the remains of two dead stars, crashing into each other to form a gamma-ray burst. The supercomputer lets one look inside the neutron stars to see what happens during the crash.

Gamma-ray bursts (GRBs) tend to come in two forms. The more common long GRBs are believed to be the first hint of a supernova, the spectacular explosion marking the death of a humongous star. These goliath stars can have as much as one hundred times more material than Earth. The more exotic short GRBs pack their whopping punch within a mere two seconds. Short GRBs are thought to come from interstellar "car crashes" of epic proportions. Besides Elon Musk's Tesla,[8] there are no cars in space. Instead of cars, the remains of two dead stars crash into one another, releasing a prodigious burst of gamma rays before a new black hole is formed.

As astronomers gazed at GRB060614, they observed many features of short GRBs despite GRB060614 lasting one hundred seconds longer than a short GRB. What's more, no one saw a supernova, not even Hubble! As a result, researchers Alon Retter and Shlomo Heller hypothesized that GRB060614 may actually be a white hole.[9] Definitive evidence for or against the white hole hypothesis must await a gravitational wave observatory to detect future events.

Wormholes may exist and provide passage to parallel universes. But where do these parallel universes come from? One theory is that white holes birth new parallel universes. Another theory considers parallel universes to be lying just beyond the edge of the universe.

Chapter Two

Beyond the Edge of the Universe

About one hundred years ago, astronomers waged the "Great Debate." On April 26, 1920, two of the top astronomers of the day debated the size of the universe.[1] In the east corner, head of the Harvard College Observatory, Harlow Shapley (1885–1972) argued that the Milky Way filled the entire universe. In the west corner, hailing from Lick Observatory in San Jose, California, Heber Doust Curtis (1872–1942) argued that the Milky Way was one among many galaxies in the universe.

Unlike a boxing match, debates in astronomy rarely have a clear knock-out winner. Astronomers at the time may have been divided on whether Shapley or Curtis carried the day. Today, astronomers unanimously agree: the Milky Way is one among hundreds of billions of galaxies in the universe. Using the Hubble Space Telescope, astronomers have observed galaxies billions of light-years away, nearly at the edge of the observable universe.[2]

The Hubble Space Telescope captured this image of spiral galaxy NGC 4622, which is located about 111 million light-years away from Earth.

In astronomy the border between the observable universe and what lies beyond is called the horizon. A horizon is the farthest distance light can stay in contact. One might think the idea of the a horizon is similar to the idea of the range of walkie-talkies. A walkie-talkie horizon would be the farthest distance two walkie-talkies could stay in contact. However, walkie-talkies have limited range due to the size and technology of the antennas. The universe's horizon is not limited by technology. Astronomers will not be able to see beyond the horizon with a larger telescope (though they will still try).

Instead, the horizon of the universe is set only by the extent to which space has expanded, which is related to the amount of time elapsed since the big bang, about 13.8 billion years. If astronomers wait another 13.8 billion years, they will be able to see galaxies at least twice as far away. Those galaxies are currently out there, beyond the universe's horizon. They are part of the universe, but not part of the observable universe. How large is the entire universe? Is it large enough that copies of our bubble universe appear? Cosmologists, who study the universe at large, give a resounding yes. But why should there exist copies of our universe? Understanding the answer to these questions requires delving into the theory of creation, the big bang theory.

Birth by Fire: The Big Bang

In 1927, a newly ordained Belgian priest, Georges Lemaître (1894–1966), published his hypothesis of the "primeval atom."[3] In his paper, Lemaître showed that his observations of the universe's expansion together with Einstein's theory of relativity required a beginning of the universe. In Lemaître's model, all the matter in the universe was once at a single point, forming a "primeval atom."

Georges Lemaître (*right*) discusses his ideas on cosmology with Albert Einstein in Pasadena, California.

During a cataclysmic event, the "atom" broke apart, forming the universe observed by astronomers today. Does this sound more like myth than science? Einstein thought so. Upon hearing Lemaître explain his theory, Einstein ferociously rejected the expansion of the universe and told Lemaître, "Your calculations are correct, but your grasp of physics is abominable."[4] To support his static universe, Einstein introduced a "fudge-factor" into his equations of relativity, which he soon thereafter called the biggest mistake of his life. Today, scientists think even Einstein's "blunders" were tremendous insights. Scientists have retained the fudge-factor, as it may explain the properties of mysterious dark energy.

The concept of an expanding universe gained acceptance a few years later, when Edwin Hubble (1889–1953), one of the greatest astronomers of all time, corroborated Lemaître's expanding universe.[5] Hubble used the largest telescope in the world and discovered that the farthest galaxies away from the Milky Way are also those racing the fastest away from the Milky Way. To understand why Hubble's discovery implies an expanding universe, just bake a loaf of raisin bread. Place the raisins evenly in the dough, perhaps an inch (2.5 cm) apart. Bake the bread and voila! The bread has expanded, displacing the raisins. Consider the raisins from the point of view of one particular raisin near the center. The neighboring raisins are now a bit farther away while the raisins near the edge are much farther away!

Although the expanding universe gained acceptance in 1929, astronomers continued to make fun of poor Lemaître. Sir Fred Hoyle (1915–2001), an eminent English astronomer, coined the phrase "big bang" while badmouthing the theory on BBC radio.[6] Hoyle supported the steady state theory, in which the universe is eternally expanding and galaxies pop up out of nowhere continuously. As strange as the steady state theory may sound, astronomers at the time found the idea of the creation of the universe in the big bang so mystical that many preferred the eternal universe of steady state theory.

It was not until Lemaître's last days that the big bang theory was finally vindicated. This wasn't exactly the "primeval atom" theory of Lemaître though. Over time, many astrophysicists reworked Lemaître's mathematics, improving the model. In

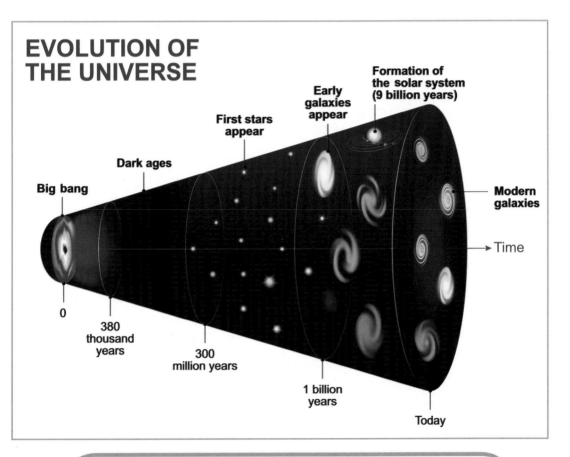

EVOLUTION OF THE UNIVERSE

Formation of the solar system (9 billion years)

Early galaxies appear

First stars appear

Dark ages

Big bang

Modern galaxies

Time

0

380 thousand years

300 million years

1 billion years

Today

This schematic of the expansion history of the universe begins with the big bang and proceeds through time (with space expanding) to today.

addition to the expansion of the universe, the modern big bang theory predicts the universe is bathed in a sea of microwaves. According to the big bang theory, the universe was initially very hot and dense. Particles of matter (protons, electrons, and many more exotic species) and particles of light (photons) were created in the first few moments after the big bang. Electrons bounced light around until the universe expanded and cooled enough for the electrons to bond with the protons to form hydrogen atoms. Free of meddlesome electrons, the leftover light from the big bang bathed the universe. As space expanded, the light stretched to the extent that the light is now, 13.8 billion years later, microwaves.

The cosmic microwave background (CMB) was a powerful prediction of big bang theory. In the early 1960s, researchers at Princeton were building radio dishes specifically to look for the CMB. Meanwhile, researchers at a nearby AT&T lab in New Jersey, Arno Penzias (1933–) and Robert Wilson (1936–), were finding annoying noise in their radio dishes.[7] Penzias and Wilson tried pointing their radio dishes in every direction, shooed birds out of the dishes, and tried everything possible to eliminate the pesky noise. They tested model after model to no avail. Just as they were beginning to despair, Penzias and Wilson heard that researchers at Princeton were building radio dishes to search for cosmic microwaves—wait a minute! Penzias and Wilson finally realized they had accidentally discovered the microwaves left over from the big bang. Fourteen years later, Penzias and Wilson won the 1978 Nobel Prize for their discovery, which ended the debate between the steady state and big bang theories for good.

Even after Penzias and Wilson's discovery of the cosmic microwave background, not everyone was happy with the big bang theory. In the past few decades, dedicated spacecraft were launched to map the temperature of the CMB, finding the early universe was much more uniform than was expected.

Why were scientists surprised the early universe was at a very nearly constant temperature throughout? Imagine being in the middle of a big Italian city square one chilly fall afternoon. In the center of the square is a fountain. The fountain is lazy, slowly spewing out its store of warm water. One would expect the water to get colder and colder as it flows farther from the source. Cosmologists expected something similar from the cosmic microwave background map. They expected nearby regions to have the same temperature, but not the entire universe!

TAKING THE TEMPERATURE OF THE UNIVERSE

In 1989, NASA launched COBE (the Cosmic Background Explorer) the first dedicated spacecraft to measure the temperature of the universe. COBE's temperature map, showing fine detail in the early universe 13.8 billion years ago, led Stephen Hawking (1942–2018) to call COBE's temperature map, "the discovery of the century, if not of all time."[8] The computing revolution in the 1990s led NASA to launch WMAP (the Wilkinson Microwave Anisotropy Probe) in 2001, fitted with the latest technology to take breathtakingly

(continued on the next page)

(continued from the previous page)

detailed temperature maps of the CMB. Based on the absence of distortions in WMAP's temperature map, cosmologists learned the universe is incredibly larger than the observable universe.

In this spherical temperature map of the cosmic microwave background taken from WMAP data, the red represents hot spots while blue represents cold spots. Each spot is roughly one millionth of a degree warmer or cooler than the average temperature; the cosmic microwave background is incredibly uniform.

Inflation Saves the Day

Imagine again the fountain. Now, suppose the water was heated in the pipes that carried the water to the central part of the fountain. Instead of the water being launched out in a fountain, suppose there was a thin chamber separating the heated water from the water above in the pool. The heated water from the pipe would rapidly spread apart to fill the chamber, which then heats the water above (the same way a hot plate in chemistry labs heats up liquids). In this case, it is no wonder every point of the pool has the same temperature. By rapidly filling the chamber, all the water in the chamber should have about the same temperature, which then evenly heats the water above.

Cosmologists think a similar answer exists explaining why the temperature throughout the universe is nearly the same. Cosmologists call this phenomenon inflation. In 1979, Alan Guth (1947–) proposed that shortly after the big bang, the universe experienced a period of rapid expansion before settling down to a more leisurely expansion rate.[9] Before such a period of inflation, every part of the observable universe was once a very tiny region of space. Just as the water in the pool was all the same temperature because it spread out from a small region very quickly, so too the universe can be at nearly the same temperature because it once occupied a very small region and expanded very quickly.

Based on detailed maps of the CMB, cosmologists think the bubble of the observable universe must be only a teeny-tiny fraction of the preinflationary universe. In such a large space, cosmologists expect there to be many clones—identical copies—of our universe. How can that be?

Take ten pennies and lay them on the floor. Group the coins into pairs. Each pair represents one universe. Now, flip pennies to try to make all five groups distinct. One should end up with something like HH, TT, HT, TH, and HT (where H is heads up and T is tails up). Two groups of pennies have the same state (HT). Those two groups represent clone universes, since they have exactly the same information.

The real universe has a mind-numbing 10^{80} states (that's eighty zeros after the one, or one hundred million, trillion, trillion, trillion, trillion, trillion, trillion). Those states describe the position, speed, and type of every particle in the universe. Encoded into those 10^{80} states is every grain of sand on Earth, every person, every atom that makes up a person. Then, it is unsurprising that 10^{80} is such a mind-blowingly large number. Yet cosmologists think that space is so large that there should be way more than 10^{80} universes beyond the horizon of the observable universe. In that case, there should be universes exactly the same as ours. In those universes, the entire history of humanity has played out the exact same way.

The idea of clone universes may seem strange, but inflation is cosmologists' best theory for solving problems of the big bang theory. What's more, clone universes are one of the tamer predictions of inflation. A variant of inflation, eternal inflation, predicts a whole ensemble of universes called the multiverse.

Chapter Three

Eternal Inflation

Although inflation solved many big problems plaguing the big bang theory, several issues remain. First, the strength of gravity is not explained. If the strength of gravity was even a tiny bit stronger, the universe would have collapsed back to nothingness before any stars, galaxies, or people were ever born. On the other hand, if the strength of gravity was a miniscule amount weaker, the universe would have expanded so rapidly that no stars, galaxies, or people could have formed.

Second, the cosmological constant (describing the strength of dark energy) is perplexingly tiny. Cosmologists observe a staggeringly small value of 10^{-122} (that's 0.000...1 with 121 zeros after the decimal).[1] If the cosmological constant was one zero larger, the universe would have expanded so rapidly that it would have ripped itself to shreds only moments after the big bang.

Third, the amount of energy liberated when hydrogen fuses to form helium, which is the difference between the masses of four individual protons and a helium nucleus, is 0.7 percent. If the efficiency was 0.1 percent smaller, then fusion, which powers

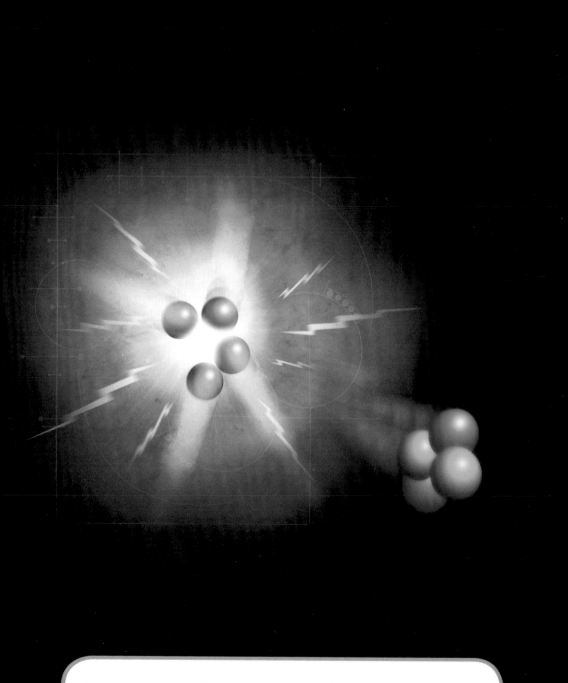

Hydrogen nuclei (four blue spheres) fuse to form helium (blue and green spheres), releasing energy in the process.

the sun, would be impossible. In that case, the universe would be a bland sea of hydrogen, unable to support carbon-based life-forms such as humankind.

Scientists call such issues fine-tuning problems. Why is it a problem that life is so exquisitely sensitive to the quantities mentioned above? Why can't scientists just accept that humanity had a lucky break? Imagine sitting on a beach on the Space Coast in Florida, waiting to watch a rocket launch. Unfortunately, the (unmanned) rocket suffers a catastrophic failure and blows up. Then a few minutes later, a hurricane sweeps through the area. The hurricane picks up all the bits and pieces of the rocket, swirling them together in its vortex before dissipating. Looking at where the hurricane once stood, one is bewildered to find the rocket has been reassembled. If a passerby grouched, "Why be shocked? Accept that it was luck," one would be yet more surprised. Surely, such a complex piece of machinery as a full-fledged rocket cannot be assembled by pure chance in such a one-off sort of event?!

In the same way, scientists feel uncomfortable when they cannot understand why a piece of physics, such as the strength of gravity, is fine-tuned. In other cases, however, scientists are less concerned about one particular event's apparent fine-tuning. Why was Houston hit by Hurricane Harvey in 2017? After all, a hurricane only hits a small segment of Texas coastline every six years on average.[2] Hurricanes typically hit other regions, so one may wonder if the conditions for Harvey to hit Houston were fine-tuned. However, 2017 was a busy year for hurricanes. Twelve hurricanes swept through the Atlantic and Eastern Pacific oceans in 2017.[3] Therefore, one may be unsurprised Houston was hit by a hurricane. Perhaps it would have been more surprising if Houston escaped 2017 hurricane-free.

What about the universe? If there are many universes, it becomes unsurprising that there exists at least one universe with the right strength of gravity. Yet, why should the other universes have different strengths of gravity?

Eternal Inflation to the Rescue

Shortly after Guth proposed his theory of inflation, it was extended by cosmologists Andrei Linde (1948–) and Paul Steinhardt (1952–).[4] They showed how the universe could gracefully exit from its period of inflationary expansion and still be consistent with the hot big bang theory. Moreover, Steinhardt demonstrated

Theoretical physicist Alexander Vilenkin is one of the most influential researchers in the development of inflation theory.

how inflation could exit in some regions (forming universes) while continuing without end in other regions. Continuing the rapid development of inflationary theory, Alexander Vilenkin (1949–) proved that Steinhardt's eternal inflation actually applies to all modern models of inflation.[5]

The work of Guth, Linde, Steinhardt, and Vilenkin, the four founders of inflationary theory, employs advanced techniques in mathematics. However, the basic ideas behind eternal inflation can be described in a beautifully simple way. Grab a pot and fill it (halfway) with water. Place the pot on a stove and turn on the heat. At first, nothing appears to happen. One

The heat from the stove increases the temperature of the water at the bottom of the pot until it boils, forming gas bubbles. The gas bubbles rise to the surface. Eternal inflation acts in an analogous way; the pot represents the multiverse, and each bubble represents a parallel universe.

can use a thermometer to show the temperature is actually increasing, yet nothing disturbs the water. However, when a liquid becomes hot enough it forms a gas, a so-called phase transition. In the pot of water, one will notice bubbles (pockets of water vapor) forming at the bottom of the pan, which then rise to the surface.

Eternal inflation operates in a similar way. The universe undergoing inflation is like the liquid water. Regions where the water became hot enough and formed bubbles are analogous to regions in the inflating universe that had a phase transition—they slowed down their inflation enough to form universes. Much as the pot forms more and more bubbles as it transitions into a roiling boil, more and more universes form out of the inflating space. Cosmologists call the collection of universes and eternally inflating space the multiverse.

Evidence for Eternal Inflation?

Since eternal inflation is a generic result for any valid theory of inflation, one could say that eternal inflation is supported by the same evidence as inflation. That is, the uniformity of the universe's temperature as observed by WMAP provides evidence for eternal inflation. Moreover, eternal inflation solves the fine-tuning problems suffered by standard inflationary big bang theory. Every bubble universe in the multiverse could have different physics, so inflation theorists say. As a result, it is unsurprising that our universe has its particular strength of gravity, and an infinite number of parallel universes in the multiverse have different strengths of gravity.

Nevertheless, many scientists find eternal inflation too far-fetched. In fact, Steinhardt, one of the founders of inflationary theory, is now one of its staunchest opponents! Steinhardt's core argument boils down to the scientific litmus test of falsifiability. A scientific theory must make particular predictions. Otherwise, it can be neither shown to be correct nor to be false. The multiverse robs inflation of any predictive power. With an infinite number of universes, one can expect anything to be true of at least one universe in the multiverse. Since the universe's properties are unknown until they are observed and eternal inflation predicts that any property can be found in some universe in the multiverse, eternal inflation predicts nothing, its critics quip.

Returning to the pot of water analogy, one may notice that bubbles can occasionally collide with one another. If our universe has collided with a parallel universe, would it have left a mark? Two groups of researchers claim to have found signs of one or more collisions in the CMB maps produced by WMAP and Planck (WMAP's successor, launched by the European Space Agency in 2009). Hopefully, their signals will prove true in future tests, but a recent case of "bad science" in cosmology (see the sidebar on the next page) urges caution.

In 2011, cosmologists at University College London, Stephen Feeney and Matthew Johnson, found "bruises" in the CMB of WMAP, in the form of four bright and dark circles.[6] Circular bruises are the expected imprint when two spheres collide with one another. The CMB appears brighter where some of the matter of the parallel universe leaks into our universe and appears darker where the matter of our universe leaks into the colliding parallel universe. Unfortunately, the circular patterns Feeney and Johnson found could also form by random chance. Finding four such signals is not strong enough evidence.

BAD SCIENCE: FALSE-POSITIVE DISCOVERY OF INFLATION

In 2014, cosmologists around the world celebrated a historic achievement: the discovery of experimental evidence for inflation. Architects of inflation Alan Guth and Andrei Linde proudly wore

A researcher works on the BICEP2 telescope.

their bibs and feasted on Swedish lobster before receiving prestigious prizes.[7] In March 2014, researchers flexing their BICEP2 (Background Imaging of Cosmic Extragalactic Polarization) telescope to its limits announced the indirect discovery of gravitational waves.[8] They observed ripples in the polarization of the CMB—that is, the direction in which cosmic microwaves swirled through space (polarized sunglasses block out light that swirls in one particular direction). A few months later, Planck sobered scientists worldwide, announcing the BICEP2 result was wrong; BICEP2 researchers incorrectly modeled the dust in the galaxy.[9] Unlike LIGO, whose researchers painstakingly checked every alternative before announcing their discovery of gravitational waves, BICEP2 researchers jumped to conclusions, leaving a deep skepticism of cosmologists' claims ever since.

Ranga-Ram Chary, a researcher of the US Planck Data Center at Caltech, used a different strategy.[10] Chary took Planck's temperature map and subtracted off a model of the CMB. Chary further subtracted off all the gas, dust, stars, and galaxies in the universe. Having removed everything from our universe, one would expect the new map to be simply noise from the detector. However, Chary found regions in the map thousands of times brighter than the expected noise levels. One explanation for Chary's bright patches is that a universe leaked matter into our universe during a collision. However, scientists urge caution. It is also possible that models of the gas and dust in the universe are incorrect. To close the case, cosmologists await a successor mission to Planck. Although the successor has not yet been named, evidence for or against eternal inflation will likely arrive far before scientists can test the multiverse of the very small: the many worlds interpretation of quantum mechanics.

Chapter Four

The Many Worlds Interpretation of Quantum Mechanics

Einstein's theory of relativity alone can explain the large-scale structure of the universe: everything from the big bang to black holes. However, at the smallest scales, strange laws of physics collectively called quantum mechanics govern the universe. The most important concept of quantum mechanics is called superposition.

In everyday life, one can easily observe classical super-position. For example, if two flashlights are pointed at the same spot, they provide a brighter light than one flashlight alone. A more vivid example of classical superposition is provided by water waves. Fill a bucket (halfway) with water. Drop a coin (or other small object such as a pebble) into the bucket. Notice the waves expanding in circles from where the coin was dropped.

After the water has settled, drop two coins at opposite ends of the bucket. At first, the waves expand from where the coins fell into the water as before. However, once the waves meet each other, things become more interesting. Waves, whether of water, sound, or anything else, are made of crests (the high points) and troughs (the low points). When two waves run into each other, a crest can lie on top of (superpose) another crest or a trough. When two crests are superposed, they add together. The water wave inches slightly higher up in those places. When a crest and a trough superpose, they cancel each other out. The water would look (momentarily) flat in that region.

The ability of waves to add and subtract when they lie on top of one another are properties of superposition called constructive and destructive interference. Constructive interference has been experienced by anyone unfortunate enough to hear the screech of a microphone. What causes the screech? When background noises (sound waves) are caught by a sensitive microphone, they are projected through a speaker. If the microphone faces the speaker, the microphone picks up the noise (again, sound waves) from the speaker it was already hearing. The two sets of sound waves will add together when they superpose, constructively interfering and getting louder and louder until the unnerving screech occurs. The process is halted by turning the microphone off or pointing the microphone away from the speaker.

Thus, classical superposition is readily experienced in daily life. Quantum superposition is quite a bit stranger, perhaps because it is never directly encountered in everyday life. According to quantum superposition, everything can be described as a sum of states (such as on and off) called the wave function. A particular state does not exist until something is

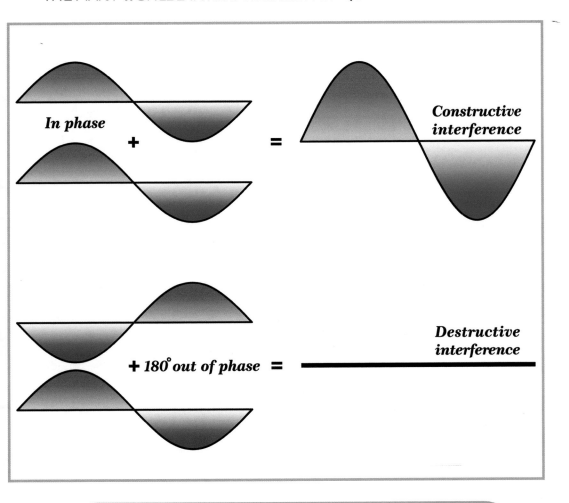

In this conceptual representation of interference, the two waves at the top are in phase (their peaks and troughs line up), so that when they interfere constructively, they add to form a stronger wave. At the bottom of the diagram, two waves are out of phase. When they are added together, they destructively interfere, canceling each other out.

observed, collapsing the wave function. For example, a coin can be described as having a heads-up state and a tails-up state. But what is the state of the coin while it is still flipping in mid-air? Quantum superposition would say the coin is both heads-up and

This visualization of Schrödinger's cat shows the cat both alive (*right*) and dead (*left*). In this case, instead of the explosive, the experiment involves a jar of poison, which if tipped over, kills the cat.

tails-up until it is observed. In this case, the coin's wave function collapses to a definite state when it falls to the ground and ends up as heads-up or tails-up.

A more complicated, though popular, example is called Schrödinger's cat. Erwin Schrödinger (1887–1961), the father of quantum mechanics, became as loathsome of quantum mechanics as his friend Einstein. After writing many letters back and forth with Einstein, Schrödinger introduced the following thought experiment in 1935.[1]

Imagine a box. In this box is a cat and an explosive. The explosive is attached to a Geiger counter with a radioactive sample. If the Geiger counter counts a radioactive decay, the explosive is set off, killing the cat. Radioactive samples are made up of atoms that may or may not decay at any given instant. Quantum superposition states that the atoms are described as decayed *and* not decayed until an observation is made. By extension, quantum superposition describes the cat as dead *and* alive. Yet, when one opens the box, the cat is alive or dead.

Supposedly, the act of observation collapses the wave function, but clearly the cat must have died before one opens the box. Otherwise, the observer would experience the explosion, too! The question of when exactly superposition ends is the point of Schrödinger's cat and is meant to convey how ridiculous the concept of a collapsing wave function is. Hugh Everett (1930–1982), who invented an interpretation of quantum mechanics without a collapsing wave function, agreed.[2]

The Quantum Multiverse

At the beginning of the 1900s, in the early days of quantum mechanics, scientists believed in the Copenhagen interpretation of quantum mechanics. According to Niels Bohr (1885–1962), eminent quantum physicist and founder of the Copenhagen interpretation, states do pop out of existence during collapse of the wave function.[3] Bohr and other quantum physicists at Copenhagen ignored Schrödinger's cat. To be fair, they didn't have any better options. In 1957, however, Everett developed the many worlds interpretation of quantum mechanics.

The simplest way to understand the many worlds interpretation is to consider a trivial choice, which is said to be in superposition until it is made. Suppose Alice and Bob are building a rocket and are writing down a list of materials. Alice asks Bob whether they should paint their rocket pink or blue. Until they make a decision, the color of the rocket exists in superposition. But for such a trivial choice, either color could be chosen. What happens to the blue state if pink is chosen? Does it simply pop out of existence as in the Copenhagen interpretation? Not at all, Everett claimed. Everett believed that every possible choice achieved reality, but in a parallel universe. In other words, when Alice and Bob make the choice to paint their rocket, the universe splits: there will be one universe in which Alice and Bob paint their rocket pink and one universe in which Alice and Bob paint their rocket blue.

In the many worlds interpretation, an infinite number of parallel universes exist. Not only do universes continually split off for every little decision a person makes (coffee or tea? Another universe), but additionally, small elements of randomness in the universe create more universes. For example, black holes slowly leak out particles, called Hawking radiation. However, the type of particle that steals the mass of the black hole is a coin toss: it could be an electron or its evil twin, a positron.

HAWKING RADIATION AND THE INFORMATION PARADOX

In 1974, Stephen Hawking leapt to the forefront of cosmology research. Black holes were so-named because they were thought to be completely dark objects from which not even light could

(continued on the next page)

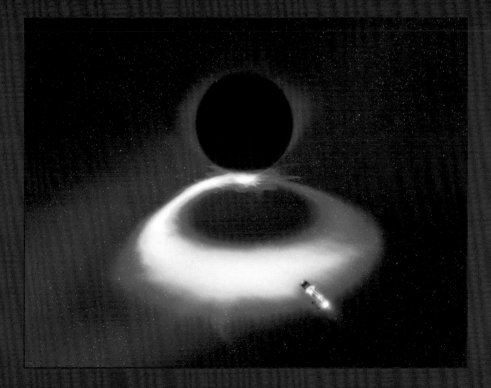

This artist's depiction shows Hawking radiation (blue glow) emanating from a black hole.

(continued from a previous page)

escape. Although it is true that light falling into a black hole cannot escape, Hawking found that the enormous gravitational energy of a black hole is slowly but steadily leached away over time, almost as though something was escaping.[4] By the quantum law of superposition, empty space can be described as a sum of particles that cancel each other out. These virtual particles can pop in and out of existence for very brief periods of time. If such a pair, say an electron and a positron, pop into existence near a black hole, one may fall into the black hole and one can float away, sapping energy from the black hole by which it was born.

Evidence for Many Worlds

The many worlds interpretation sounds utterly untestable. How could one determine if the universe splits into two for each quantum choice? Surely the Copenhagen interpretation, in which one state fades out of existence, should be preferred just because it is simpler? Strangely enough, there is a way to test the many worlds interpretation.

In 1985, David Deutsch (1953–) proposed several experiments that can distinguish between the collapse of the wave function in the Copenhagen interpretation versus the objective reality of each state in a parallel universe, the many worlds interpretation.[5] However, these experiments won't be happening any time soon! Deutsch's experiments depend upon quantum computers, machines that rely on the laws of quantum mechanics to perform

Neil Gershenfeld, a researcher at the Massachusetts Institute of Technology (MIT), stands next to a prototype of a quantum computer. Unlike regular computer bits, which can only exist as either "on" or "off," quantum bits can be on and off simultaneously.

computations exponentially faster than classical computers. A powerful quantum computer can place billions of particles in superposition repeatedly until it can tell whether a collapse of the wave function occurs (as in the Copenhagen interpretation) or not (as in the many worlds interpretation).

Although, IBM made quantum-computing technology accessible to the public in 2016, quantum computers are nowhere near powerful enough yet to perform Deutsch's experiments. The most powerful quantum computer in 2018 can use only fifty quantum-bits.[6] Modern computers can store billions of bits. Quantum computing technology is exploding, but it may be decades before Deutsch's experiment can be performed.

Chapter Five

Hyperspace: A Fifth Dimension?

Imagine, once again, the paper world of Papias. In particular, suppose the paper child Papias was a doodle on the piece of paper. As such, Papias would only have knowledge of what existed in Paper Town. A pencil or an eraser nearby would be completely inconceivable to residents of the paper world. If in fact a human were to erase the ice cream store in Paper Town, the paper people would be flummoxed. The erasure could only be regarded as an act of God.

Suppose, however, some meddlesome human stuck a pencil through the piece of paper. Suppose the resulting rip was in a remote part of the piece of paper, far away from the houses and stores in Paper Town so no paper people were harmed. Similar to the punch holes, many paper people perished jumping into the rip. One day, a daredevil motorcycle rider, Paper Danger, arrived on the scene. Paper Danger wanted to set the new Paper Town record for most airtime in a motorcycle jump. Revving up the motorcycle's engine, Paper Danger took off on the motorcycle, traveling faster up the rip than any paper person had before. Paper Danger launched up high and above the paper world, spinning the motorcycle over and around in a death-defying spiral. During this epic airtime, Paper Danger saw the eraser and pencil just beyond Paper Town. The idea of the pencil causing the rip came to Paper Danger's mind. Sticking the landing on the opposite side of the rip, Paper Danger tried to explain the strange three-dimensional world beyond Paper Town. Unfortunately, the paper people had no concept of a land beyond Paper Town and thought Paper Danger was delirious from the jump.

In a similar way, some scientists wonder if there is a fifth dimension, while other scientists scoff and call such an idea ludicrous. Nonetheless, experimental evidence for a fifth dimension may arrive in the not so distant future. But before exploring the possibility of a fifth dimension, it is useful to consider the fourth dimension.

Space-time

From the story of Paper Danger, one can understand how difficult people find understanding the fourth dimension. After all, humankind is constrained to living in a three-dimensional world. It took more than two hundred years from the time Sir Isaac Newton (1643–1727) wrote his law of gravitation, distinguishing space and time, before Einstein married the two together, introducing the concept of space-time in his theory of relativity.

One can simplify the concept of space-time by plotting space on the x-axis and time on the y-axis on a graph. Such a plot is called a space-time diagram. Scientists do this since it is difficult enough to represent three dimensions on a piece of paper, let alone four! In a space-time diagram, a person sitting still is a

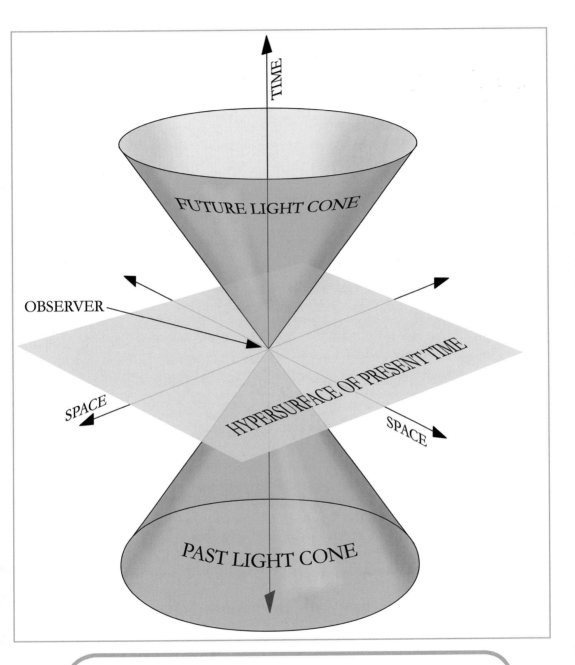

This space-time diagram with light cones shows all possible future paths an object could take, with the most angled paths (45°) only taken for objects traveling at the speed of light. An observer's worldline is vertical (if stationary) or imperceptibly close to vertical if moving.

vertical line, since their position in space remains constant while time steadily marches on. Lines in a space-time diagram, such as the vertical line of a person sitting, are called worldlines. How would one draw Usain Bolt's worldline during his 2016 gold medal 100-meter sprint? One might expect the worldline should be nearly horizontal. It could be, depending upon the stretch of the x-axis and y- axis. But traditionally, the worldline of a photon, a particle of light, is a diagonal line, 45° from the x-axis. According to Einstein's theory of relativity, the speed of light is the speed limit of the universe: nothing can travel faster. In that case, it is impossible for a worldline to have an angle less than 45° on a space-time diagram (unless they use the fifth dimension as in 2018's *A Wrinkle in Time*). Surprisingly, Usain Bolt's 100-meter worldline would be hardly distinguishable from a person sitting. How can that be? The speed of light is a whopping 671,080,888 miles (1,080,000,000 kilometers) per hour. Usain Bolt ran about 22 miles (35.4 km) per hour, nearly one-millionth of a percent of the speed of light, which is also one-millionth of a degree from the vertical line.

TESSERING ACROSS THE UNIVERSE

In the film *A Wrinkle in Time* (2018), three children use a tesseract to travel instantaneously billions of light-years across the universe. In a space-time diagram, their worldlines would momentarily be gigantic horizontal lines. What is a tesseract? In physics and mathematics, a tesseract is a means of representing four dimensions while only using three dimensions. It uses perspective in a similar manner to how an artist can add the impression of a third dimension to a two-dimensional painting. In *A Wrinkle in Time*, a tesseract is a little bit different. In the film, a tesseract is a means of using the fifth dimension to connect two distant points in the universe.

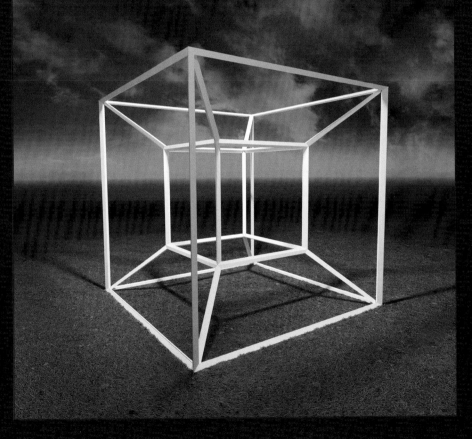

This tesseract represents the four-dimensional version of

Hyperspace and Beyond

After studying the space-time diagrams of four dimensions, one may wonder again about a fifth dimension. Is there any basis for believing a fifth dimension exists? Two researchers in the 1920s gave a resounding yes. Shortly after Einstein published his four-dimensional theory of relativity, Theodor Kaluza (1885–1954) and Oskar Klein (1894–1977) unified Einstein's theory of gravitation with Maxwell's laws of electromagnetism by supposing there exists a fifth dimension.[1,2] Why has no one noticed the fifth dimension? Kaluza and Klein supposed the extra dimension was tightly curled up next to the other dimensions, to the extent that it is not normally noticeable (being billions of billions times thinner than a hydrogen atom).

Yet, as Jedi-master Yoda would say, size matters not. The existence of a fifth dimension can explain puzzles plaguing physics. A long-standing issue in four-dimensional physics ponders: if light can travel through empty space and light is a wave, then what is waving? For water waves, the water is waving. For sound waves, the air is waving. Historically, scientists thought space must be filled with some material, which they called the aether. Otherwise, how can light wave through space? Experiments that led Einstein to publish his radical theory of relativity proved the aether does not exist. Yet the question of how light can wave through empty space remains in the four-dimensional universe. In a five-dimensional universe, the answer becomes shockingly simple: light waves are vibrations in the fifth dimension.

An additional motivation for believing in a fifth dimension is to understand quantum entanglement, a bizarre phenomenon of quantum mechanics. Einstein himself showed that quantum

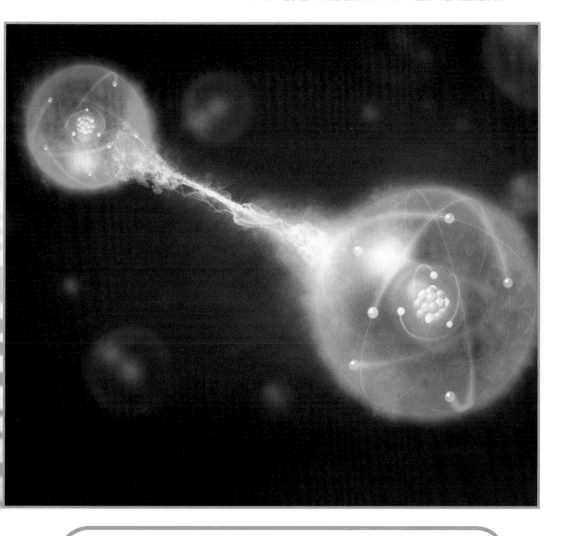

This artistic interpretation of quantum entanglement shows two atoms (red spheres) being connected across space and time.

mechanics requires groups of interacting particles to share the same state, even if they are separated by a large distance.[3] In other words, if a scientist makes an observation of the state of one particle, that observation instantaneously collapses the wave function of the other particle. The two particles are said to be entangled, which Einstein derogatorily called "spooky action at a distance." Similar to Schrödinger's cat, Einstein meant to show that quantum mechanics is so bizarre it must be wrong. It would seem the universe is too strange for even the brightest physicist. In 1982, French physicist Alain Aspect (1947–) performed an experiment convincingly showing that quantum entanglement exists.[4] Nevertheless, Einstein need not despair. If there is a fifth dimension, quantum entanglement can exist without being "spooky action at a distance." Instead, the entangled particles share the same state because they are linked by the fifth dimension.

The wave nature of light and quantum entanglement give theoretical reasons for believing a fifth dimension exists. However, is there any experimental evidence for the fifth dimension? Not yet. Scientists may be able to find evidence for a fifth dimension using enormous particle collider experiments, such as the Large Hadron Collider (LHC) in Geneva, Switzerland. In 2013, the LHC wowed the world by discovering the Higgs boson, a particle that explains why objects in the universe are heavy rather than weightless.[5] However, finding evidence for a fifth dimension requires a much higher energy particle collision than was used to find the Higgs boson. Why? How does one detect evidence for the fifth dimension in the first case?

An additional, theoretical reason for believing there exists a fifth dimension is that it explains why gravity is so much weaker than the other forces (hence why refrigerator magnets can stick to a refrigerator rather than fall to the ground). Gravity controls the shape of the universe. Thus, if there exists a fifth dimension, the gravitational force will be "spread thin" compared to the other forces that only operate in the usual four-dimensional space-time. If the gravitational field truly is spread thin by a fifth

A visitor stands in front of an image of the Large Hadron Collider at the Science Museum in London, England. Each of the metallic objects is a massive magnet, whose purpose is to accelerate particles to extreme energies.

dimension, particle collisions of enormous energy can interact with the gravitational field stretching in the direction of the (albeit tremendously small) fifth dimension.[6] Evidence of this interaction can be found from the energy, type, and direction of the new particles produced.

If the LHC was too weak to find the fifth dimension, what will it take to do so? That depends: the smaller the fifth dimension is the higher energy particle collision is required. If the fifth dimension is not too small, the LHC may even find evidence for it in the next few years. Shortly after discovering the Higgs boson, the LHC was powered down. During the following two years, teams of scientists and engineers upgraded the machine, making it twice as powerful. Each winter the machine has been upgraded, but there are no signs of the fifth dimension in the data yet. Evidence for a fifth dimension could be found in the next few years or not until the successor of the LHC, which could unimaginatively be named the Extra Large Hadron Collider (XLHC). Even if we find evidence for a fifth dimension, why can't there be more?

Chapter Six

Strings and Branes: Eleven Dimensions

Scientists in the twentieth century became infatuated by the notion of higher dimensions. Leaping on the success of Kaluza and Klein, researchers wondered if adding yet more dimensions would complete the dying wish of Einstein, uncovering the holy grail of physics: a theory of everything. The result of hundreds of scientists' efforts is indeed a candidate theory of everything. They have found a theory wedding relativity, which governs the universe at the largest scales, with quantum mechanics, which governs the universe at the smallest scales. The theory remains in development as it currently lacks a necessary ingredient of scientific theories, falsifiability. As the theory has developed, its name has grown more and more esoteric, evolving from superstring theory to M-theory.

NOT EVEN WRONG?

M-theory remains an incomplete theory as it predicts a "landscape" of 10^{500} possible universes. The number 10^{500} is so outrageously large, it can hardly be comprehended. Puny by comparison, there are only 10^{22} (10 billion trillion) grains of sand on Earth, only 10^{44} (100 million trillion trillion trillion) molecules of sand on Earth, and only 10^{80} (100 million trillion trillion trillion trillion trillion trillion) particles in the universe. As such, searching for our universe amongst the 10^{500} possibilities is more difficult than finding a needle in a haystack the size of the universe. For the same reasons as eternal inflation, with so many possibilities, M-theory is not falsifiable, compelling critics to scorn that it's "not even wrong." Although 10^{500} is nigh impossible to understand, it's not impossible to write down:

100000000000000000000000000000000000000000000000000
00000000000000000000000000000000000000000000000000000
00000000000000000000000000000000000000000000000000000
00000000000000000000000000000000000000000000000000000
00000000000000000000000000000000000000000000000000000
00000000000000000000000000000000000000000000000000000
00000000000000000000000000000000000000000000000000000
00000000000000000000000000000000000000000000000000000
00000000000000000000000000000000000000000000000000000
00000000000000000000000000000000000000000000000000000
000000000000000000000000000000000000000000000000

In a nutshell, superstring theory is actually quite simple. Take a piece of string and wrap it up tightly into a tiny ball. If one walks far enough away from the balled-up string it becomes impossible to tell there is anything more than a dot. In the same way, electrons, protons, photons, every supposedly point particle in the universe is modeled as being an incredibly small bundle of strings. If all particles are strings, how can one tell them apart? Why are electrons negative and have weight while photons, particles of light, are neutral and have no weight? One could ask the same question of why plucking different strings on a guitar produces different musical notes. After all, each guitar string is still a string! While this is true, the strings of a guitar have different tensions, thickness, and weight, producing different notes. In a similar way, the strings making up different particles vibrate differently and the vibrations set the charge and mass of the particle.

To account for both relativity and quantum mechanics, superstring theory requires the existence of ten dimensions, five more than the theory of Kaluza and Klein. String theorists are not afraid of higher dimensions (earlier, less successful models considered twenty-six dimensions), but they were disappointed until the 1990s when five separate superstring theories seemed equally likely to be the true theory. The second revolution of string theory was launched in 1995 when Edward Witten (1951–) suggested that the five superstring theories could be unified into a single theory if one supposed the universe consists of eleven dimensions.[1] Witten named the resulting theory M-theory, where M was meant as a placeholder standing for mystery, magic, or membrane depending upon personal preference, until the theory is completed and a suitable name can be chosen. As it stands, M-theory may require decades more work by thousands of scientists before it may become a finished theory.

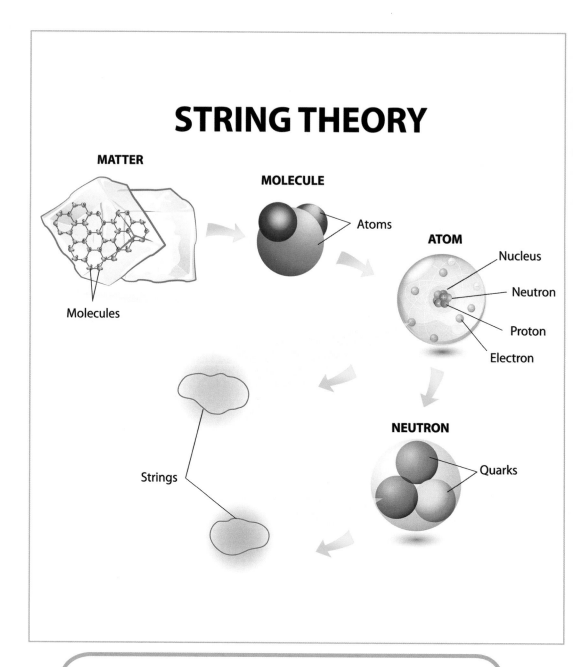

STRING THEORY

A large-scale object, such as an ice cube, is made up of molecules; molecules are made of atoms; the insides of atoms are made of quarks; and quarks are made of strings. Strings are the most basic building block of the universe, according to string theory.

Hidden in Plain Sight?

In M-theory, where are all those extra dimensions? One model follows the reasoning of Kaluza and Klein by supposing the extra dimensions are so tightly curled around four-dimensional space-time that they cannot ordinarily be noticed. Imagine a garden hose. The hose is clearly three-dimensional in someone's hand. However, if that person walks far away from the hose, it will look like a line, which is one-dimensional. Similarly, scientists can explore the three-dimensional nature of the sun with orbiting spacecraft, but from Earth, telescopes see only a two-dimensional disk. Furthermore, stars are so incredibly distant that they appear as points, zero-dimensional objects. But when one studies close-up images of a star, one can see that the star is actually a ball of hot gas, which is a three-dimensional object. What all this means is that the farther away an object is, or the smaller the object is, the lower its dimensionality appears to be.

Thus, the extra dimensions in M-theory may be extremely tiny and impossible to detect without the help of advanced technology. This explanation was appealing to scientists in the past two decades because it seemed the LHC should be able to prove the existence of the extra dimensions. By colliding particles at sufficiently high energies, interactions with the curled-up dimensions would become evident. The LHC has still not detected any evidence for the existence of curled-up extra dimensions, making some scientists nervous the curled-up dimensions simply don't exist. On the other hand, a different model, the brane and bulk model, supposes the extra dimensions make up parallel universes.

Stars seen from Earth are so distant that they appear to be points of light—zero-dimensional objects.

Branes in a Bulk

Branes are utterly bizarre objects, with a name appropriately suggesting that they are difficult to define in simple language. Branes are generalizations of dimensional objects. This is easier to understand by example. The generalization of a point particle is a zero-dimensional brane, the generalization of a string is a one-dimensional brane, and the generalization of a 2D surface is a membrane. In the brane and bulk model, the three space dimensions of our universe make up one "three-brane" in the

This artistic rendering shows the universe being created from two branes (higher dimensional surfaces that the universe lies on) colliding with one another. The huge amount of energy released from the collision eventually forms particles that in turn form galaxies and stars.

bulk, the system of branes. One could also call the bulk the multiverse, but string theorists use the word "bulk" to separate their theory from the multiverse of eternal inflation. String theorists theorize that there exist at most two other "three-branes" similar to our universe and at least one dimension of time. In the brane and bulk model, the big bang was caused by a collision between branes floating in the bulk, and the model predicts inflation did not occur.[2] Steinhardt, who was one of the founding fathers of inflation, is now one of the staunchest proponents of this alternative to inflation, called the ekpyrotic model. Since there is no inflation, future experiments can falsify the ekpyrotic model if evidence for inflation is found.

In either case, new ranks of scientists are needed to continue the charge. As much has been learned about parallel universes in the hundred years since Einstein published his theory of relativity, many more questions are waiting to be solved.

CHAPTER NOTES

Chapter 1.
Wormholes in Space-time

1. John Michell, "VII. On the Means of Discovering the Distance, Magnitude, &c. of the Fixed Stars, in Consequence of the Diminution of the Velocity of Their Light, in Case Such a Diminution Should Be Found to Take Place in Any of Them, and Such Other Data Should Be Procured from Observations, as Would Be Farther Necessary for That Purpose," *Philosophical Transactions of the Royal Society London* 74 (January 1, 1784): p. 35.

2. Albert Einstein and Nathan Rosen, "The Particle Problem in the General Theory of Relativity," *Physical Review* 48, no. 1 (July 1, 1935): p. 73.

3. Robert W. Fuller and John A. Wheeler, "Causality and Multiply Connected Space-time," *Physical Review* 128, no. 2 (October 15, 1962): p. 919.

4. Élie Cartan, "Sur une généralisation de la notion de courbure de Riemann et les espaces à torsion," *Comptes rendus de l'Académie des Sciences* 174 (1922): p. 593.

5. Denis Sciama, "The Physical Structure of General Relativity," *Reviews of Modern Physics* 36, no. 1 (January 1, 1964): p. 463.

6. Tom Kibble, "Lorentz Invariance and the Gravitational Field," *Journal of Mathematical Physics* 2 (March–April 1961): p. 212.

7. Neil Gehrels et al., "A New γ-ray Burst Classification Scheme from GRB 060614," *Nature* 444 (2006): p. 1044.

8. Steve Spaleta, "Observatory Spots Elon Musk's Tesla Roadster Zooming Through Space (Video)," Space.com,

February 9, 2018, https://www.space.com/39647-spacex-tesla-roadster-spotted-in-space.html.

9. Alon Retter and Shlomo Heller, "The Revival of White Holes as Small Bangs," arxiv.org, accessed April 18, 2018, https://arxiv.org/pdf/1105.2776v1.pdf.

Chapter 2.
Beyond the Edge of the Universe

1. "Why the 'Great Debate' Was Important," NASA, accessed April 18, 2018, https://apod.nasa.gov/htmltest/gifcity/cs_why.html.

2. "The Hubble Deep Fields," Hubble Space Telescope, accessed April 18, 2018, http://www.spacetelescope.org/science/deep_fields/.

3. Georges Lemaître, "Un Univers homogène de masse constant et de rayon croissant rendant compte de la vitesse radiale des nébuleuses extragalactiques," *Annales de la Société Scientifique de Bruxelles* A47 (1927): p. 49.

4. J. J. O'Connor and E. F. Robertson, "Georges Henri-Joseph-Edouard Lemaître," University of St. Andrews, Scotland, July 2008, http://www-history.mcs.st-andrews.ac.uk, http://www-history.mcs.st-andrews.ac.uk/Biographies/Lemaitre.html.

5. Edwin Hubble, "A Relation Between Distance and Radial Velocity Among Extra-galactic Nebulae," *Proceedings of the National Academy of Sciences of the United States of America* 15, no. 3 (March 15, 1929): p. 168.

6. Walter Sullivan, "Fred Hoyle Dies at 86; Opposed 'Big Bang' but Named It," *New York Times,* August 22, 2001, http://www.nytimes.com/2001/08/22/world/fred-hoyle-dies-at-86-opposed-big-bang-but-named-it.html.

7. "Penzias and Wilson Discover Cosmic Microwave Radiation 1965," PBS, 1998, http://www.pbs.org/wgbh/aso/databank/entries/dp65co.html.

8. Edward Goldstein, "John C. Mather: NASA's Nobel Laureate," NASA, updated August 6, 2008, https://www.nasa.gov/50th/50th_magazine/matherInterview.html.

9. Alan Guth, "Inflationary Universe: A Possible Solution to the Horizon and Flatness Problems," *Physical Review D* 23, no. 2 (January 15, 1981): p. 347.

Chapter 3.
Eternal Inflation

1. John D. Barrow and Douglas J. Shaw, "The Value of the Cosmological Constant," *General Relativity and Gravitation* 43, no. 10 (May 16, 2011): p. 2555.

2. David Roth, "Texas Hurricane History," National Weather Service, updated January 17, 2010, http://www.wpc.ncep.noaa.gov/research/txhur.pdf.

3. "2017 Eastern Pacific Hurricane Season," National Hurricane Center, accessed April 18, 2018, https://www.nhc.noaa.gov/data/tcr/index.php?season=2017&basin=epac.

4. Andreas Albrecht and Paul J. Steinhardt, "Cosmology for Grand Unified Theories with Radiatively Induced Symmetry Breaking," *Physical Review Letters* 48, no. 17 (April 26, 1982): p. 1220.

5. Alexander Vilenkin, "Birth of Inflationary Universes," *Physical Review D* 27, no. 12 (June 15, 1983): p. 2848.

6. Stephen M. Feeney, Matthew C. Johnson, Daniel J. Mortlock, and Hiranya V. Peiris, "First Observational Tests of Eternal Inflation," *Physical Review Letters* 107 (July 12, 2011): p. 071301.

7. Max Tegmark, "Good Morning, Inflation! Hello, Multiverse!" *HuffPost,* updated December 6, 2017, https://www.huffingtonpost.com/max-tegmark/good-morning-inflation-he_b_4976707.html.

8. P.A.R. Ade et al. (BICEP2 Collaboration), "Detection of *B*-Mode Polarization at Degree Angular Scales by BICEP2," *Physical Review Letters* 112 (June 20, 2014): p. 241101.

9. R. Adam et al. (Planck Collaboration), "Planck Intermediate Results: XXX. The Angular Power Spectrum of Polarized Dust Emission at Intermediate and High Galactic Latitudes," *Astronomy & Astrophysics* 586 (2016): p. A133.

10. Ranga-Ram Chary, "Spectral Variations of the Sky: Constraints on Alternate Universes," *The Astrophysical Journal* 817, no. 1 (2016): p. 33.

Chapter 4.
The Many Worlds Interpretation of Quantum Mechanics

1. Rachel Feltman, "Schrödigner's Cat Just Got Even Weirder (and Even More Confusing)," *Washington Post,* May 27, 2016, https://www.washingtonpost.com/news/speaking-of-science/wp/2016/05/27/schrodingers-cat-just-got-even-weirder-and-even-more-confusing/?utm_term=.d7b6327ffb89.

2. Hugh Everett III, "Theory of the Universal Wavefunction," thesis, Princeton University, (1956): pp. 1–140.

3. Werner Heisenberg, *Physics and Philosophy* (New York, NY: Harper & Brothers, 1958), p. 125.

4. Stephen Hawking, "Black Hole Explosions?" *Nature* 248 (March 1974): p. 30.

5. David Deutsch, *Quantum Concepts of Space and Time*, eds. Roger Penrose and C.J. Isham (Oxford, UK: The Clarendon Press, 1986), p. 204.

6. Will Knight, "IBM Raises the Bar with a 50-Qubit Quantum Computer," MIT Technology Review, November 10, 2017, https://www.technologyreview.com/s/609451/ibm-raises -the-bar-with-a-50-qubit-quantum-computer/.

Chapter 5.
Hyperspace: A Fifth Dimension?

1. Theodor Kaluza, "Zum Unitätsproblem in der Physik," *Sitzungsberichte der Königlich Preussische Akademie der Wissenchaften Berlin* (1921): p. 966.

2. Oskar Klein, "The Atomicity of Electricity as a Quantum Theory Law," *Nature* 118 (October 9, 1926): p. 516.

3. Albert Einstein, Boris Podolsky, and Nathan Rosen, "Can Quantum-Mechanical Description of Physical Reality Be Considered Complete?" *Physical Review* 47, no. 10 (May 15, 1935): p. 777.

4. Alain Aspect, Philippe Grangier, and Gérard Roger, "Experimental Realization of Einstein-Podolsky-Rosen-Bohm *Gedankenexperiment*: A New Violation of Bell's Inequalities," *Physical Review Letters* 49, no. 2 (July 12, 1982): p. 91.

5. S. Chatrchyan et al. (CMS Collaboration), "Observation of a New Boson at a Mass of 125 GeV with the CMS Experiment at the LHC," *Physics Letters B* 716, no. 1 (2012): p. 30.

6. Bryan Webber, "How to Find the Fifth Dimension," Cavendish Laboratory, Cambridge, accessed April 18, 2018, www.hep. phy.cam.ac.uk/theory/webber/RStalk.ps.

Chapter 6.
Strings and Branes: Eleven Dimensions

1. Edward Witten, "String Theory Dynamics in Various Dimensions," *Nuclear Physics B* 443 (March 24, 1995): p. 85.

2. Justin Khoury, Burt A. Ovrut, Paul J. Steinhardt, and Neil Turok, "The Ekpyrotic Universe: Colliding Branes and the Origin of the Hot Big Bang," *Physical Review D* 64 (August 15, 2001): p. 123522.

GLOSSARY

big bang The event by which time and space began to exist.

black hole A region of space where gravity is so strong that not even light can escape.

brane A generalization of a dimensional object, for example, the generalization of a point particle is a zero-dimensional brane, and the generalization of a string is a one-dimensional brane.

bulk The higher dimensional space our universe inhabits, according to the brane and bulk model.

horizon The farthest distance light can stay in contact.

hyperspace A set of more than three spatial dimensions.

inflation A period of time shortly after the big bang during which the universe rapidly expanded.

multiverse The collection of all universes inflated after the big bang.

parallel universe Any universe that exists separate from our universe.

quantum entanglement The phenomen that occurs when groups of particles separated by a large distance interact and share the same state.

quantum mechanics Laws of physics that explain the smallest things in the universe.

relativity Laws of physics that explain the most extreme environments.

superstring theory A theory that strings are the most basic building block of the universe.

wormhole A hypothetical structure that connects two different points in space or time.

FURTHER READING

Books

Bartusiak, Marcia. *Black Hole: How an Idea Abandoned by Newtonians, Hated by Einstein, and Gambled on by Hawking Became Loved*. New Haven, CT: Yale University Press, 2015.

Blumenthal, Kelly. *Cosmic Inflation Explained.* New York, NY: Enslow Publishing, 2018.

Conlon, Joseph. *Why String Theory?* Boca Raton, FL: CRC Press, 2016.

Gaughan, Richard. *Wormholes Explained.* New York, NY: Enslow Publishing, 2018.

Hilton, Lisa. *The Theory of Relativity*. New York, NY: Cavendish Square Publishing, 2016.

Merali, Zeeya. *A Big Bang in a Little Room: The Quest to Create New Universes*. New York, NY: Basic Books, 2017.

Websites

Lawrence Berkeley National Lab: Inflation for Beginners
aether.lbl.gov/www/science/inflation-beginners.html
Astrophysicist John Gribbin explains in detail the flatness problem and how inflation solves it before describing more surprising predictions of inflation.

NASA Science: The Big Bang
science.nasa.gov/astrophysics/focus-areas/
what-powered-the-big-bang
This NASA webpage explains in greater detail the cosmic microwave background (CMB) from the big bang and the spacecraft whose mission it was to make temperature maps of the CMB.

Nova: Relativity and the Cosmos
www.pbslearningmedia.org/resource/phy03.sci.phys.fund.
relandcosmos/relativity-and-the-cosmos
Explore the history behind Einstein's discovery of general relativity, along with an outline of the theory and its implications.

INDEX